Give and Take

Dana Carroll

Rigby
A Harcourt Achieve Imprint

www.Rigby.com
1-800-531-5015

My brother has a bike with two wheels.
I hope I get a bike with two wheels, too.

3

Mom says that I can have a new bike.
But first I have to do some work.
I put away my jump rope.

5

I help my sister.
Mom says, "Thank you for your help."

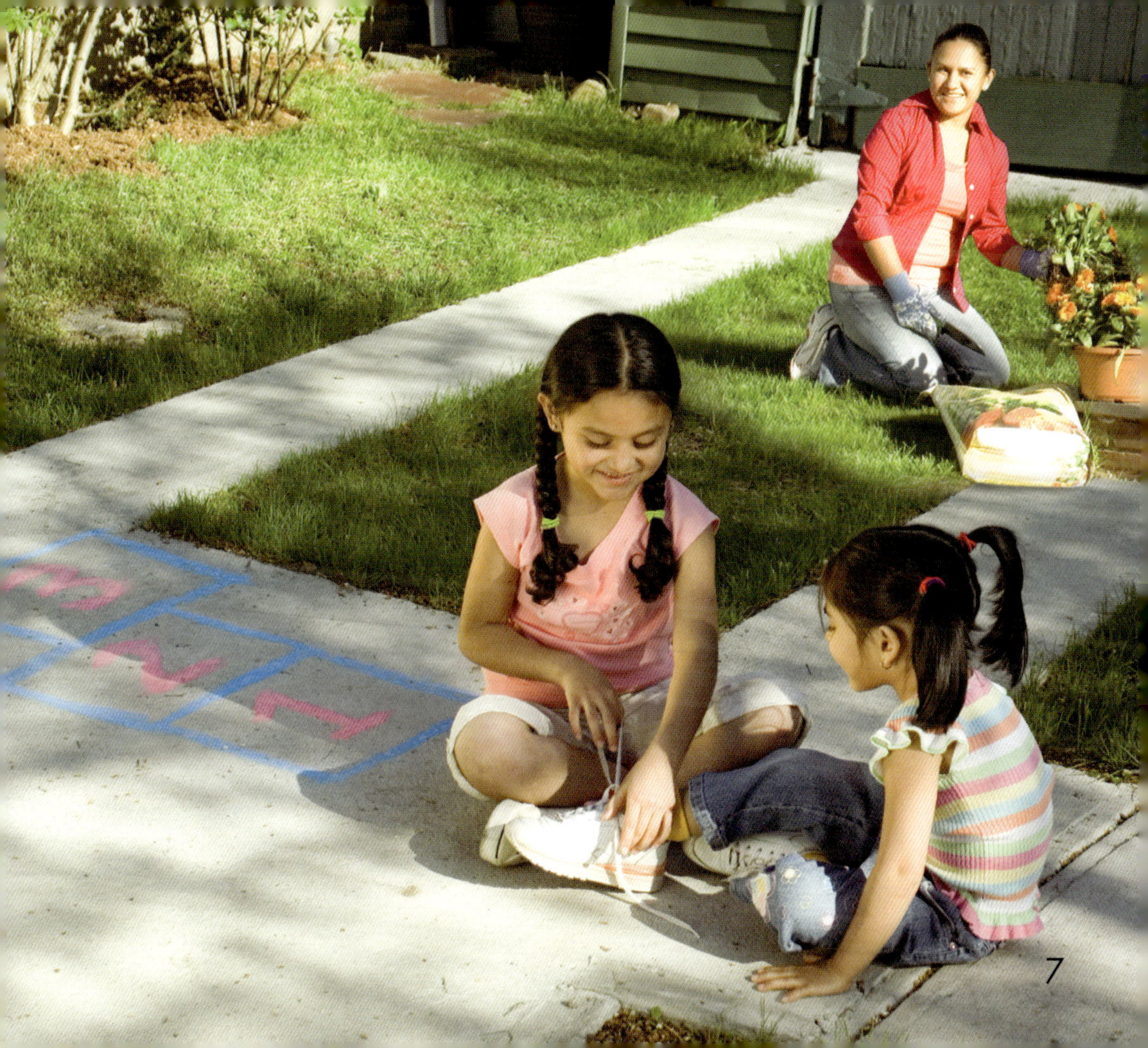

Then I help Dad.
Dad says, "Thank you for your help."

9

My brother's plane broke.
So I let him use my new ball.
He says, "Thank you for the ball."

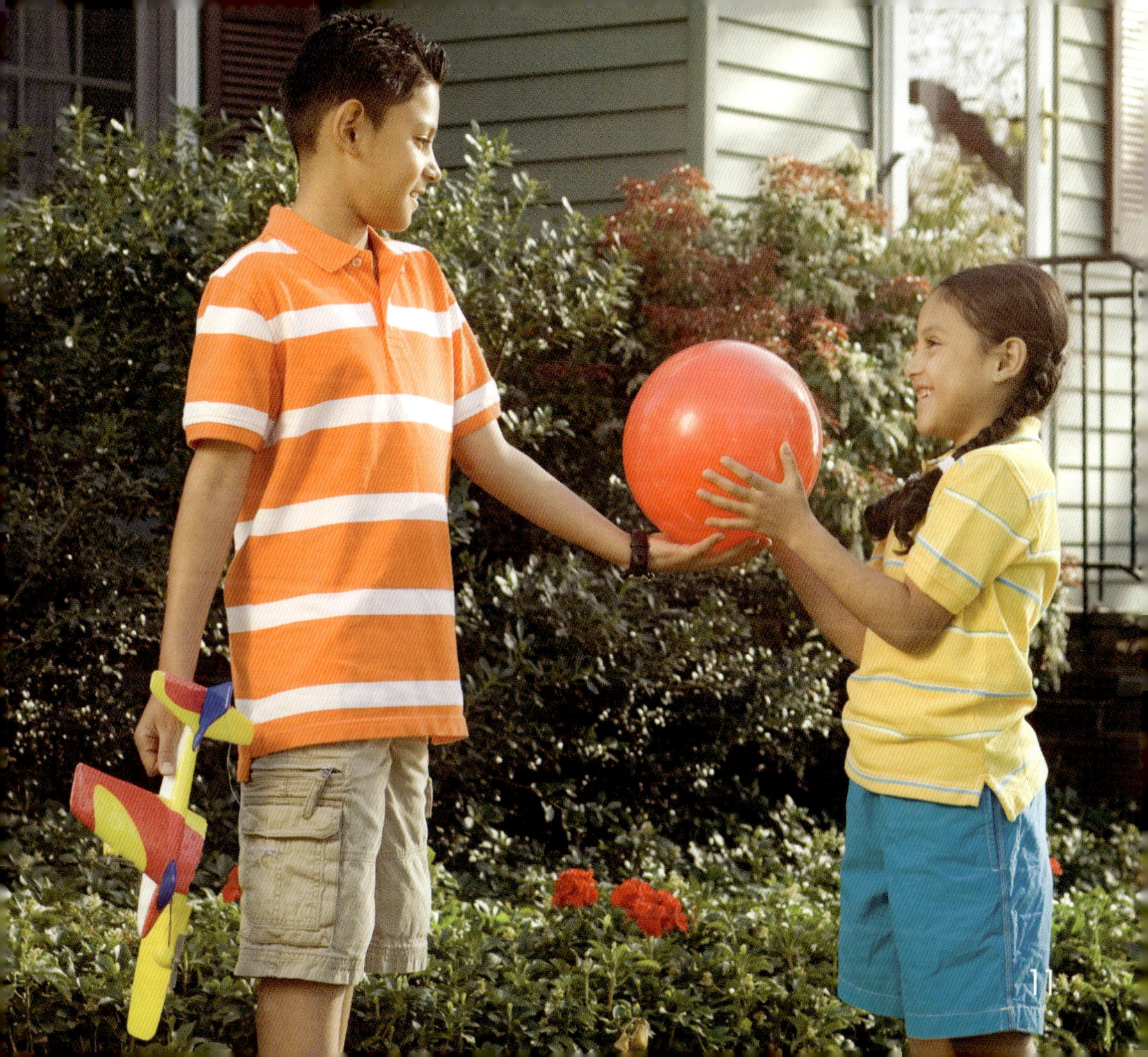

One day Dad gives me a new bike with two wheels. I say, "Thank you for the bike!"

Then Dad takes my old bike.
Dad says, "Thank you for your bike."

That is what it means to give and take.